Jacob Adam Kappey

Songs of Scandinavia and Northern Europe

A collection of 83 national and popular songs of Russia, Poland, Lithuania, Finland, Sweden, Norway, Denmark, and Holland

Jacob Adam Kappey

Songs of Scandinavia and Northern Europe
A collection of 83 national and popular songs of Russia, Poland, Lithuania, Finland, Sweden, Norway, Denmark, and Holland

ISBN/EAN: 9783337298845

Printed in Europe, USA, Canada, Australia, Japan

Cover: Foto ©Thomas Meinert / pixelio.de

More available books at **www.hansebooks.com**

SONGS

OF

SCANDINAVIA

AND

NORTHERN EUROPE.

A COLLECTION OF

83

NATIONAL AND POPULAR SONGS

OF

RUSSIA,

POLAND, LITHUANIA, FINLAND,
SWEDEN, NORWAY, DENMARK, AND HOLLAND,

WITH ENGLISH WORDS BY

CLARA KAPPEY,

EDITED BY

J. A. KAPPEY.

BOOSEY & CO.,
295, REGENT STREET, LONDON, W.,
AND
9, EAST 17th STREET, NEW YORK.

PREFACE.

In making this collection of National Songs of Northern Europe the Editor's aim has been to select, not only from the musical literature of our own time examples of the Songs of the most popular composers of Scandinavia and Russia, but to add also some of the many ancient characteristic Melodies belonging to these regions.

It will be readily understood that the selection of some eighty specimens from the vast material at hand, consisting of the songs of seven distinct nationalities, has been by no means an easy task. The Editor, however, cherishes the hope that he may be instrumental in directing the lover of National Songs to a comparatively new field, full of interest.

The translations have been made as close to the originals as idiomatic peculiarities and the exigencies of musical rhythm permitted

J. A. K.

INDEX.

RUSSIAN SONGS.

NAME OF SONG		PAGE	NAME OF SONG		PAGE
Russian National Anthem	A. von Lvoff	1	Turtle Dove (the) ... Old Song		51
At the window	A. Warlamoff	3	Parting Sorrow ... „		52
Stay! oh stay!	„	6	Soldier's Farewell (the) ... „		53
Ah! tell me why	„	8	**POLISH SONGS.**		
Tears	„	10			
Wanderer's Night Song	„	12	Polish National Song		54
Peace	„	14	Mazurek: "See the sun yonder" Old Song		57
Parting's Sorrow	„	16	Tell me now, my little darling „		58
Nightingale (the)	Alibieff	19	Laura to Filon „		59
Oh pray!	A. Markewitsch	22	Make a bargain ... „		60
Friendship	A. Derfeldt	24			
Gipsy's Song (the)	A. von Lvoff	26	**LITHUANIAN SONGS.**		
Oh! tell it her	L. Kotschonbey	28			
Forsaken	Dargomijsky	30	Daina: "To the Lark" ... Ancient Song		61
Jamschick's Complaint (the)	Bachmetieff	32	Daina: "The Bride's Farewell" „		62
Talisman (the)	Titoff	34			
Cossack's Lullaby (the)	Bachmetieff	38	**FINNISH SONGS.**		
Cossack's Song (the)	J. C. Grünbaum	42			
Cossack (the)	Ukrainian Song	45	Rune: "Tho' from Poets" ... „		63
Three-in-band	Petersburg Air	48	Wilt thou soon return? ... L. Rocke		66
Three-in-hand	Moscow Air	50			

SWEDISH SONGS.

National Song: "Charles John"	Du Puy	68	No more with yearning	L. Rocke	108
Midst roses sweet	H.R.H. Prince Gustav of Sweden & Norway	70	Beggar-boy (the)	Old Song	110
			Orphan (the)	„	111
Courting	Lindblad	74	Sorrow's Might	Ancient Ballad	112
Summer evening (a)	„	77	Little Katie	„	116
Sparrow (the)	„	78	Dancing Song, from Dalecarlia "Come, oh fairest maiden"	Old Melody	118
On the mountain	„	80			
Young Postillion (the)	„	84	Dalecarlian March: "Brave of heart and warriors bold"	„	120
Old Age	„	90			
Ah! my sad song dies away	„	92	**NORWEGIAN SONGS.**		
Disappointed expectation	„	94			
Silvio to Laura	„	96	To rest I call ye lambkins all ... Old Song		122
Ever near	„	98	Abandoned		124
Joy	„	100	Guldterning		126
Suspicion	„	102	Reindeer Song		127
Afar	„	104			
Missive unto her I'll send (a)	L. Rocke	107			

DANISH SONGS.

National Song: "King Christian"	Hartmann	123	Fly, birdie, fly!	I. P. E. Hartmann	144
Dannebrog (the)	National Song	132	Little Karen	P. Heise	146
Denmark, by whose verdant strand	R. Bay	135	Knight's courtship (the)	Old Song	148
			Journeyman's Song	N. P. Hillebrand	149
Denmark	C. F. Weyse	138	By the sea shore	Niels W. Gade	150
Soldier brave (a)	Hornemann	140	Farewell, darling Maggie	Niels W. Gade	155

DUTCH SONGS.

National Song		158	Patriots (the)	Old Song	174
Flanders	Richard Hol	160	Merry Maidens (the)	„	176
William of Nassau	A.D. 1568	162	Flemish maiden and Frenchman	Flemish Song	178
Tithe (the)	A.D. 1570	164	Little flower (a)	W. F. G. Nicolai	180
Dutch Ballad	15th Century	168	Little witch (the)	W. F. G. Nicolai	182
Gay Fisherboy (the)	16th Century	170	My heart's belov'd is mine	W. F. G. Nicolai	186
Greek Huntsman (the)	Old Legend	172			

The Russian National Anthem.

At the window.
(RUSSIAN SONG.)

Music by A. WARLAMOFF.

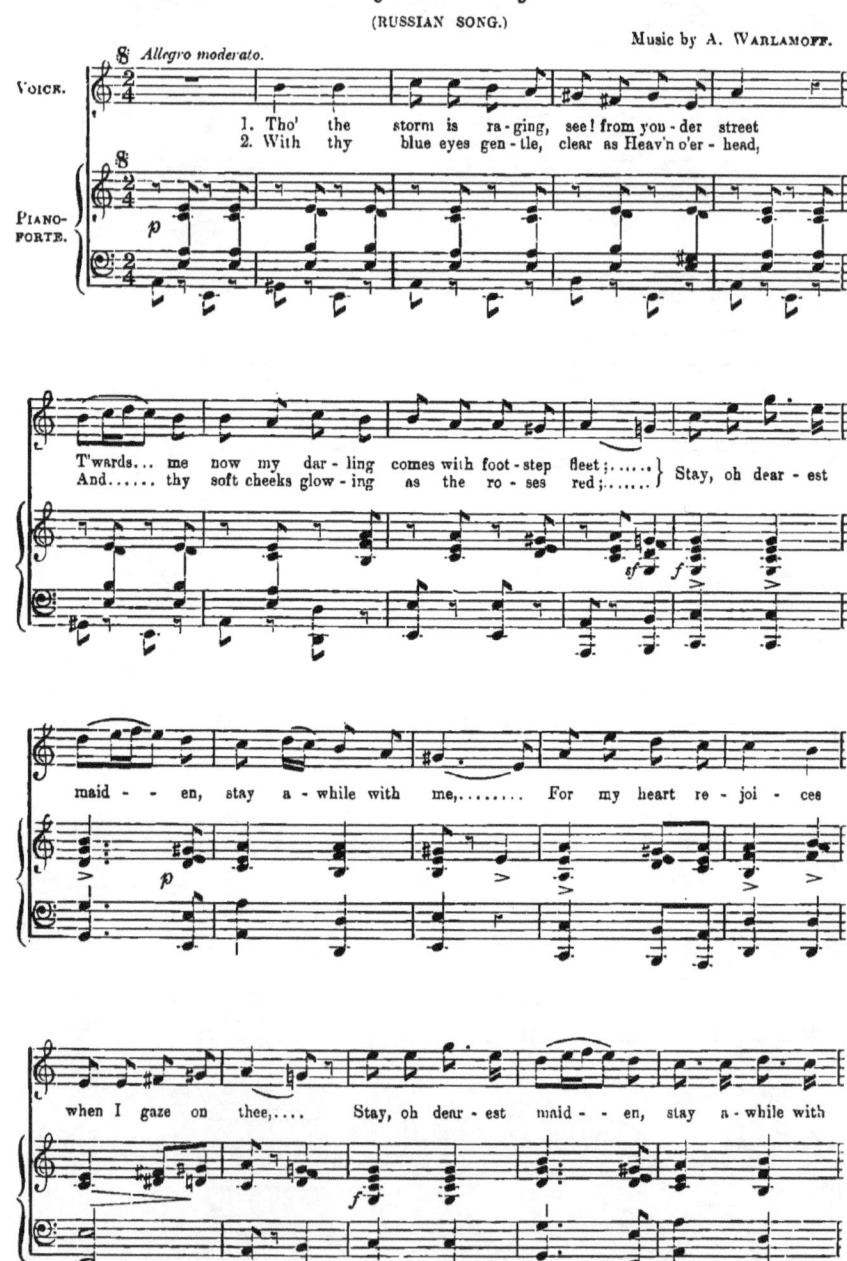

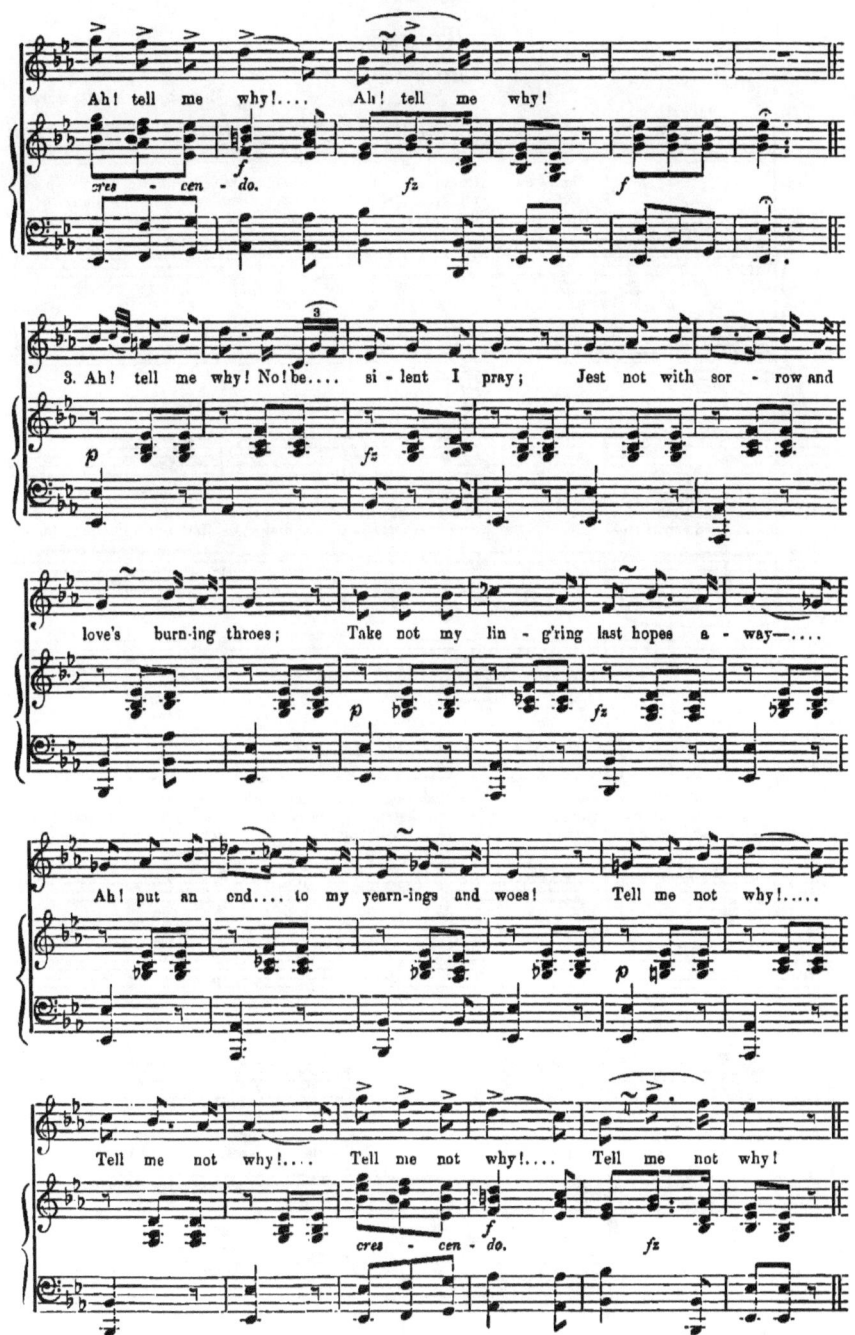

Wanderer's Night Song.

(RUSSIAN SONG.)

Music by A. Warlamoff.

Parting's Sorrow.

(RUSSIAN SONG.)

Music by A. Warlamoff.

Oh pray!

(RUSSIAN SONG.)

Music by A. Markewitsch.

The Gipsy's Song.

(RUSSIAN SONG.)

Music by A. Lvoff.

The Cossack's Lullaby.

(RUSSIAN SONG.)

Music by N. BACHMETIEFF.

THE COSSACK'S LULLABY.

The Cossack's Song.
(RUSSIAN SONG.)

J. O. Grünbaum.

THE COSSACK'S SONG.

*** A Collection of Songs and Duets by ANTON RUBINSTEIN, the most prominent of Russian composers, is published in two volumes of the "Royal Edition."

The Cossack.
(OLD RUSSIAN SONG OF UKRAINE.*)

* Ukraine, or Kharkof, is the name of a province of "Little Russia," on the banks of the Dnieper. This song refers to the enrollment of a recruit into the ranks of the "Don Cossacks," who are considered to belong to the élite of the army of Russia.

Three-in-hand.

(MOSCOW AIR.)

The three-in-hand is slow-ly roll-ing From town to town o'er lev-el road; A lit-tle bell is sad-ly toll-ing, Hard by with-in the dark... pine wood, A lit-tle bell is sad-ly toll-ing Hard by with-in the dark pine wood.

The Turtle Dove.

(OLD RUSSIAN SONG.)

Parting Sorrow.

(OLD RUSSIAN SONG.)

The Soldier's Farewell.

(OLD RUSSIAN SONG.)

Polish National Song.

* Skrzynecki, (pronounce Skrshe-netz-key,) a Polish officer, was intrusted by the Polish National Parliament, during the struggle of that nation for liberation from the Russian yoke, (1830—31) with the command-in-chief of the national forces. Skrzynecki gained some brilliant victories over the Russian armies (March to August, 1831, but the fruits of his successes were lost by his unaccountable hesitation in prosecuting them to the end. The suspicion that he temporised with the Russians for his own ends led the National Parliament to institute a court of inquiry into his generalship. He then resigned the chief command, after holding it for the brief period of about 8 months, during which his victories had raised the nation's hopes to the highest point.

POLISH NATIONAL SONG.

Mazurek.*

(POLISH SONG.)

* The striking similarity of this old melody with the initial phrase of the air "Wenn auch die Wolke sie verhülle," in the opera 'Der Freischütz," leads one to think that Weber knew and adapted this strain.

Laura to Filon.
(POLISH SONG.)

To the Lark.

(LITHUANIAN DAINA.*)

* *Daina*, (pl. Dainos,) Lithuanian term for *secular* song, in contradistinction to *Gėsmė—sacred* or religious song.

Finnish Rune.*

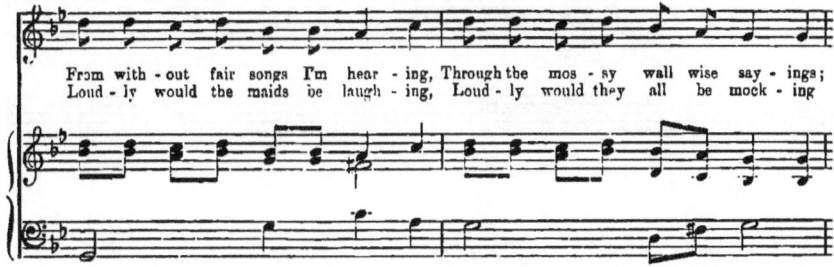

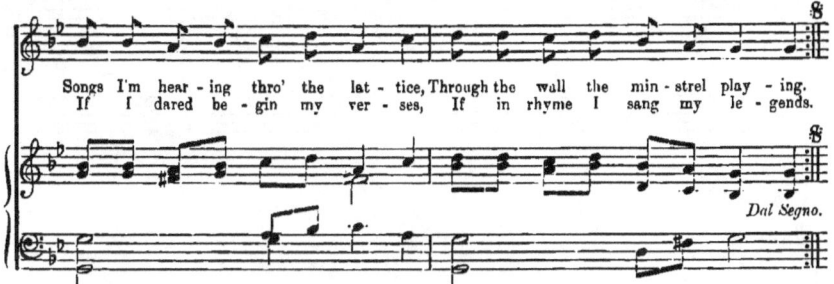

---

* Runa, Run, (pronounce Roon.)—ancient North European word, signifying "song," or "speech"; Runo, "air," or "ballad." On popular holidays the widely scattered inhabitants of Finland assemble at well-known meeting-places, when target firing, wrestling, and *extemporaneous singing of Runes* form the staple amusements.
    In the old *traditional Runas*, which have been preserved through centuries by oral transmission, the deeds of the heroes of the North, as well as the legends of the Northern Mythology are related. In the *extemporaneous Runa* of our time, important events in family life are mostly the subjects; or they may be the result of a public competition, in which both women and men take part. On these occasions the Runa forms the vehicle by which peculiarities or frailties of individuals are turned into ridicule.
    The *Magic Runa* was believed to possess great powers of evil, and an old Finnish law, dating from the time when Christianity was introduced into these countries, prohibits the singing of Magic Runes or other witchcraft under punishment of exile. The above example gives a fair idea of the semi-barbaric glow of imagination which characterises this class of songs.

SWEDISH SONGS.

Charles John.*

(SWEDISH NATIONAL SONG.)

Music by Du Puy.

* The original consists of six verses, the contents of which are condensed here to four.

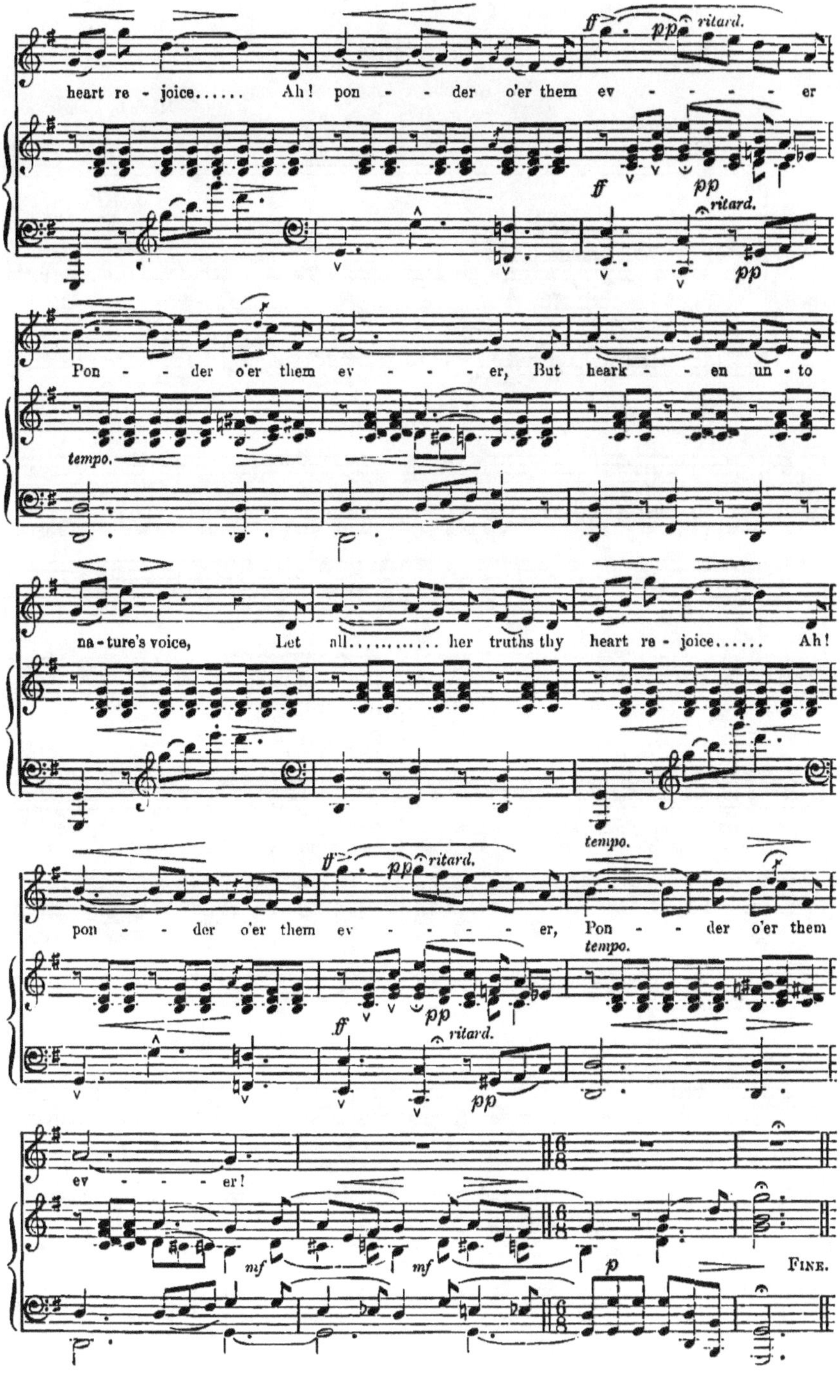
ff pp ritard.
heart re - joice...... Ah! pon - - der o'er them ev - - - - - er
ff pp ritard. pp
Pon - - der o'er them ev - - - - er, But heark - - en un - to
tempo.
na - ture's voice, Let all........... her truths thy heart re - joice...... Ah!
tempo.
ff pp ritard.
pon - - der o'er them ev - - - - - er, Pon - - der o'er them
tempo.
ff pp ritard. pp
ev - - - er!
mf mf p
Fine.

A summer evening.

(SWEDISH SONG.)

Music by LINDBLAD.

The Sparrow.

(SWEDISH SONG.)

Music by LINDBLAD.

On the mountain.

(SWEDISH SONG.)

Music by Lindblad.

The young Postillion.

(SWEDISH SONG.)

Music by Lindblad.

THE YOUNG POSTILLION.

Old Age.

(SWEDISH SONG.)

Music by LINDBLAD.

Disappointed expectation.

(SWEDISH SONG.)

Music by LINDBLAD.

Silvio to Laura.

(SWEDISH SONG.)

Music by LINDBLAD.

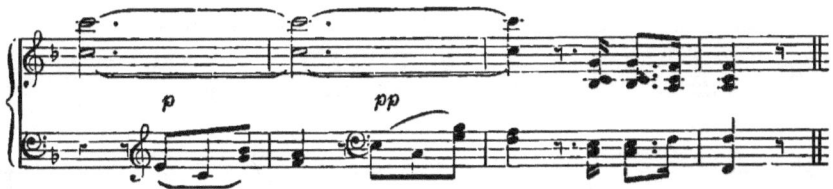

Ever near.

(SWEDISH SONG.)

Music by A. F. LINDBLAD.

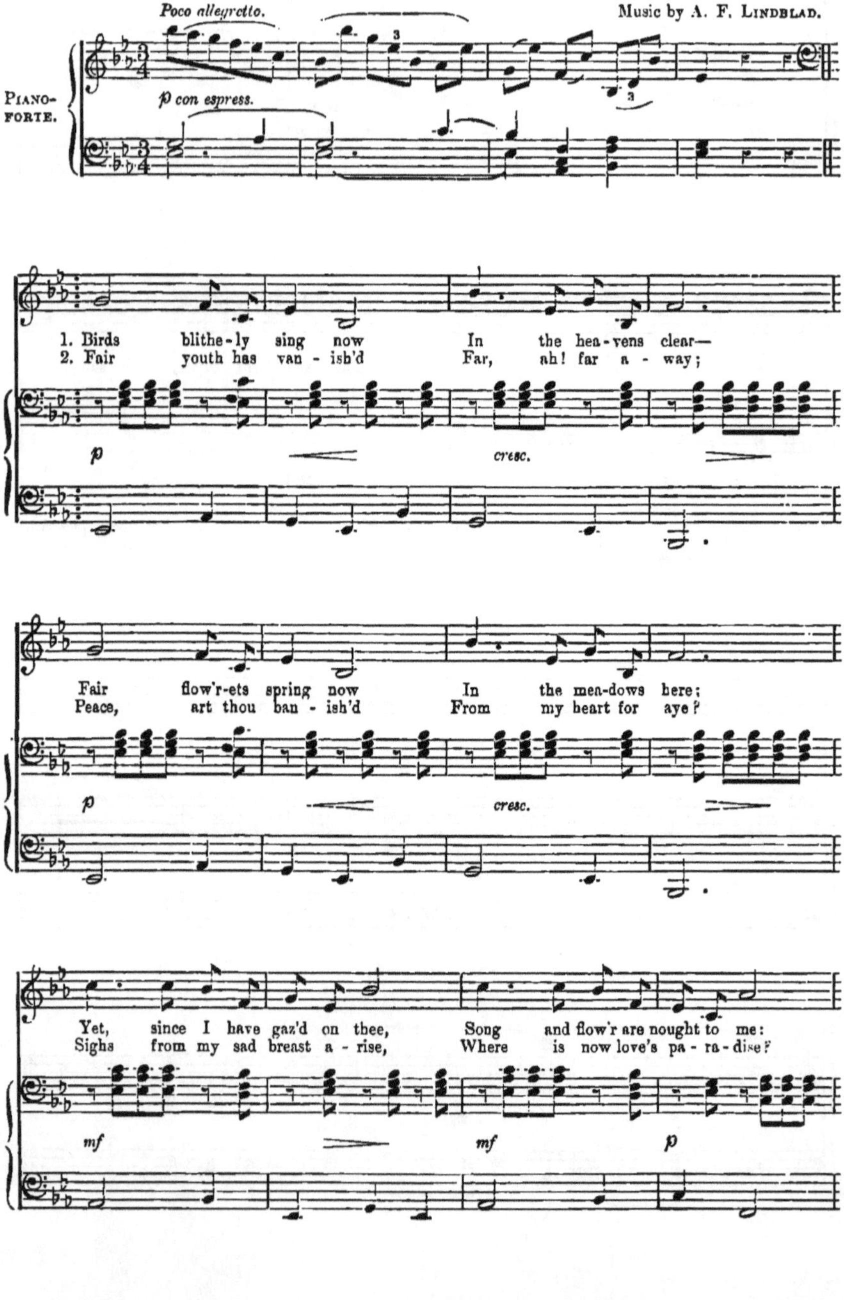
Poco allegretto.
PIANO-FORTE.
p con espress.
1. Birds blithe-ly sing now In the hea-vens clear—
2. Fair youth has van-ish'd Far, ah! far a-way;
p
cresc.
Fair flow'r-ets spring now In the mea-dows here;
Peace, art thou ban-ish'd From my heart for aye?
p
cresc.
Yet, since I have gaz'd on thee, Song and flow'r are nought to me:
Sighs from my sad breast a-rise, Where is now love's pa-ra-dise?
mf
mf
p

JOY.

Suspicion.

(SWEDISH SONG.)

Music by Lindblad.

Afar.

(SWEDISH SONG.)

Music by Lindblad.

A missive unto her I'll send.

(SWEDISH SONG.)

Arranged by L. Rocker.

1. A missive unto her I'll send, That she, alas, may know What woes my yearning bosom rend, Since she afar did go. Why should mine eye stray round me e'er? Her form it seeks in vain! Without her I for nothing care, Each joy is mix'd with pain!
2. Ah! if I roam thro' wood and dale, Thine image haunteth me, When sings the thrush, or nightingale, It warbles but of thee! Why sheds the rose her sweet perfume, Bloom lilies on my way? For me one flow'r alone can bloom For ever and for aye!
3. Oft think I of the hour, dear love, When we were forc'd to part, The stars gleam'd bright in heav'n above, And we were heart to heart. The quail-cry sounded on the air, And seem'd "farewell" to sigh. No words can tell our dark despair, As we two said "good-bye!"
4. As long as the sun each day to turn Again towards the west, E'en so for thee my heart does yearn, Within my aching breast. Oh! be thou true to me my love, I love on earth but thee! And while on earth I live and move, My heart will faithful be.

The Orphan.

(OLD SWEDISH SONG.)

Little Katie.

(ANCIENT SWEDISH BALLAD.)

Come, oh fairest maiden!

(SWEDISH DANCING SONG, FROM DALECARLIA.*)

* Dalecarlia, or Dalarne, a province of Sweden, consisting of the mountainous land lying round the Dal-elf.

Brave of heart and warriors bold.

(DALECARLIAN MARCH.)

To rest I call ye lambkins all.

(NORWEGIAN SHEPHERDS' SONG.)

Abandoned.

(NORWEGIAN SONG.)

Guldterning.*

(NORWEGIAN SONG.)

1. Thou love-ly maid-en come and throw the gold-en dice with me. Ah! I pos-sess no yel-low gold to stake in play with thee. The gold-en dice they throw, the gold-en dice they throw to-geth-er.
2. What mat-ter if thou have no gold to spend or lose in play? Right glad-ly I for stakes will fix thy young heart fresh and gay.
3. The dice are thrown; the first time they up-on the ta-ble fall, The maid-en los-es;—strange to say she does not scold at all!

* A northern game of dice.

Reindeer Song.

(LAPLANDISH SONG.)

DANISH SONGS.

King Christian.
(DANISH NATIONAL SONG.)

Music by Hartmann.

* *Skiold*, the son of Odin, from whom the race of the Skioldinger descend.

The Dannebrog.*

(DANISH NATIONAL SONG.)

Music by BAY.

1. Proud Dan-ne-brog be flow-ing O'er Co-dan's roll-ing flood. Night can-not hide thy glow-ing, Oh ban-ner red as blood! For thee has brave-ly striv-en, And fall-en many a knight, Dear Denmark's name t'wards hea-ven, Wav'd high thy cross of light.

2. To us thou cam'st from hea-ven, Dear re-lic of the Dane. Bold sons for thee have striv-en, Their glo-ry ne'er shall wane. Thy name a-broad is ring-ing, Far o-ver land and sea; While north-ern bards are sing-ing Shall live the praise of thee!

* Prompted by Pope Gregory IX, King Valdemar the Conqueror undertook an expedition to Esthonia for the purpose of converting the heathens there to christianity, 1219. The Danes were almost defeated, when, (as states the legend,) the *Dannebrog*-banner fell from heaven, and raised them to victory. This saying undoubtedly arose from the fact that the Pope gave Valdemar for this undertaking a "holy banner."—blood red, with a white cross in the centre—which became later the Danes' chief standard in all their wars, till it was lost to them in the unfortunate expedition to Ditmarsh in 1500.

Denmark.

(DANISH PATRIOTIC SONG.)

Music by C. F. Weyse.

A Soldier brave.

(DANISH NATIONAL SONG.)

Music by HORNEMANN.

1. As I to war did go, As I to war did go, My maid-en would come too, yes, My maid-en would come too. That can-not be, my love, For ev-er on we move, And if no ball does hit me, why, Soon home a-gain I'll rove. Ah! were the foe not near,.. I ne'er to war would go; Yet all the Dan-ish maid-ens now

2. The two old ones you see, The two old ones you see, Thus spake they un-to me, yes, Thus spake they un-to me: "If all our men now go To fight a-gainst the foe, Ah! who will plough for us our fields, And who the grass will mow? Yes, that is just the rea-son why we must march, hurrah! Or else will come the Ger-mans and*

* German-Danish war, regarding the annexation of Sleswig-Holstein to Prussia.

* North German dialect for "shut up!"

Fly, birdie, fly!

(DANISH SONG.)

Music by I. P. E. HARTMANN.

Farewell, darling Maggie.

(DANISH SONG.)

Music by NIELS W. GADE.

DUTCH SONGS.

Dutch National Song.

1. Let him in whom old Dutch blood flows, Un-taint-ed, free and strong; Whose heart for Prince and coun-try glows, Now join us in our song; Let him with us lift up his voice, And sing in pa-triot band, The song at which all hearts re-joice, For Prince and Fa-ther-land, For

2. We bro-thers, true un-to a man, Will sing the old song yet; A-way with him who ev-er can His Prince or land for-get! A hu-man heart glow'd in him ne'er, We turn from him our hand, Who cal-lous hears the song and pray'r, For Prince and Fa-ther-land, For

Flanders.*

Music by Richard Hol.

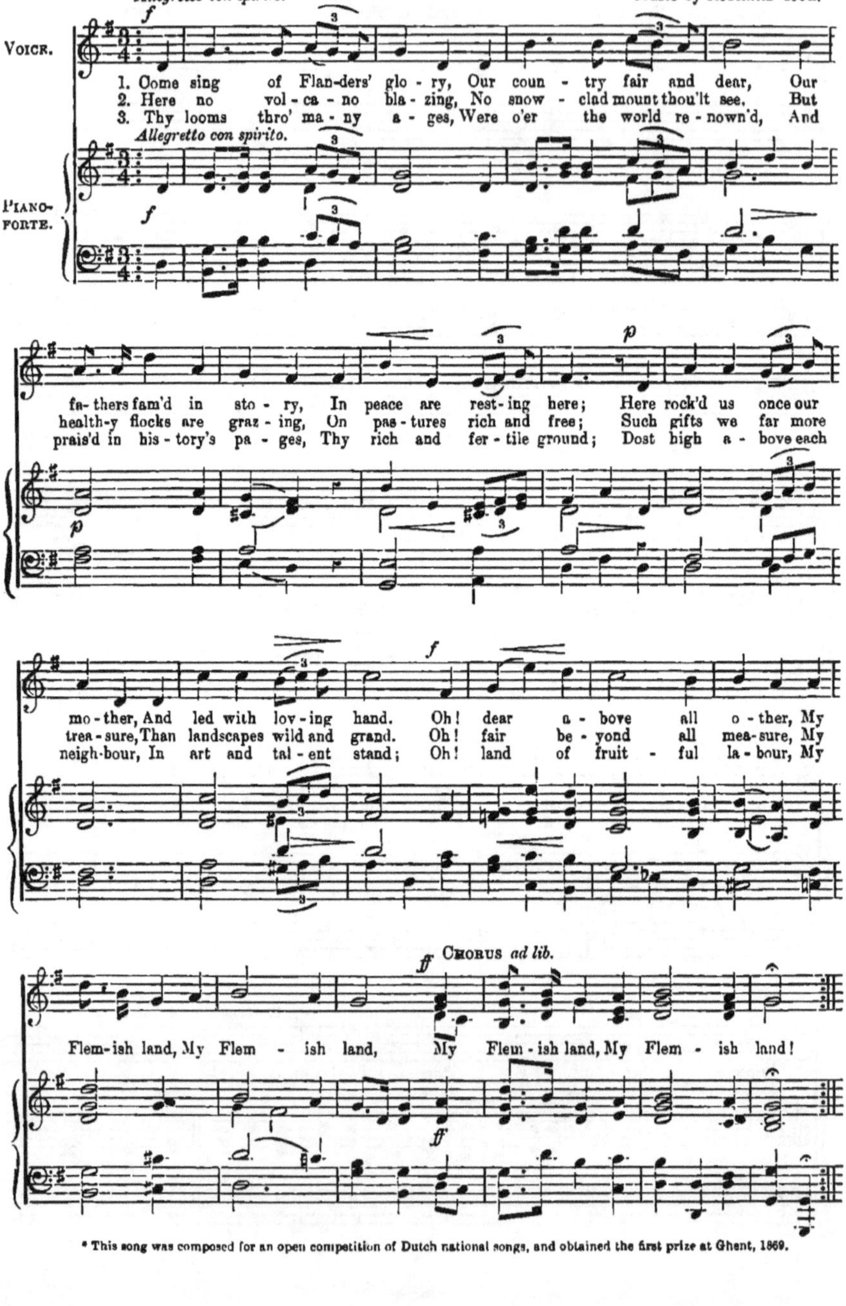

1. Come sing of Flan-ders' glo - ry, Our coun - try fair and dear, Our fa- thers fam'd in sto - ry, In peace are rest-ing here; Here rock'd us once our mo-ther, And led with lov-ing hand. Oh! dear a - bove all o - ther, My Flem-ish land, My Flem - ish land, My Flem - ish land, My Flem - ish land!

2. Here no vol - ca - no bla - zing, No snow - clad mount thou'lt see. But health-y flocks are graz - ing, On pas - tures rich and free; Such gifts we far more trea - sure, Than landscapes wild and grand. Oh! fair be - yond all mea-sure, My Flem-ish land, &c.

3. Thy looms thro' ma - ny a - ges, Were o'er the world re - nown'd, And prais'd in his - tory's pa - ges, Thy rich and fer - tile ground; Dost high a - bove each neigh-bour, In art and tal - ent stand; Oh! land of fruit - ful la - bour, My Flem-ish land, &c.

* This song was composed for an open competition of Dutch national songs, and obtained the first prize at Ghent, 1869.

# William of Nassau.
(DUTCH PATRIOTIC SONG. A.D. 1568.)

1. Of Nas-sau, and O-ra-nia, A true Dutch prince am I; The crown of fair His-pa-nia I ev-er hon-our'd high; My Fa-ther-land I guard-ed With mild and faith-ful hand; Yet now...... I am dis-card-ed, Am robb'd of crown and land!

2. My faith in God nought's mov-ing, I know that I.. shall reign, If He's of me ap-prov-ing, O'er my dear land a-gain. Oh, Neth-er-lands, to save ye, My life, my all, I'd yield, As brave...... A-dol-phus gave ye His life on Fries-land's field!

* "William of Nassau," and "The Tithe," are good specimens of a numerous class of Dutch songs which owe their origin to the time when the Duke of Alva was sent to the Netherlands, armed by Philip II., with the most absolute power over the unhappy country, to mercilessly extinguish the rising flame of religious reformation and political independence. In the admirable work of J. F. Williams, "Oude Vlaemsche Liederen, ten deele met de Melodiën," Ghent, a number of these lyrics are preserved. Unfortunately they are nearly all of great length, "William of Nassau" consists of 15 verses, which the length of this work forbids to give in full; though greatly condensed, the version given here preserves the sense of the whole.

The Tithe.*

(OLD DUTCH PATRIOTIC SONG. A.D. 1570.)

* See footnote to previous song.

Old Dutch Ballad.*

* The original Ballad contains 11 verses, which are here condensed into five. This melody is evidently a variation of the German Lied, "In einem kühlen Grunde."

The gay Fisherboy.

(OLD FLEMISH SONG.)

16th Century.

* This allusion to "leather shoes" indicates a sort of dandyism, being a luxury rarely indulged in by the working classes of those days.

The Patriots.

(DUTCH SONG.)

The merry Maidens.
(DUTCH SONG.)

THE MERRY MAIDENS.

The Flemish maiden and the Frenchman.

(FLEMISH SONG.)*

1. Fare-thee-well, my Flem-ish maid-en, 'Gainst my will must I de-part; Ah! be-lieve me, tho' I quit thee, I with thee shall leave my heart. Yet thou'lt have an-o-ther lov-er, Ere one lit-tle week be past,.. E-ven now the troops of
2. "Tho' I am a Flem-ish maid-en, Sons of France I love full well; I have giv'n my gal-lant sol-dier, More to thee than words can tell. Nev-er shall a for-eign troop-er Have the love I gave to thee,.. Thou art dear-er, oh! be-

* This song has been skilfully introduced by Lortzing, in his opera of "Czar and Zimmermann."

THE FLEMISH MAIDEN AND THE FRENCHMAN.

The little witch.

(MODERN DUTCH SONG.)

Music by W. F. G. Nicolai.

My heart's belov'd is mine.

(MODERN DUTCH SONG.)

Music by W. F. G. Nicolai.

THE
IMPERIAL EDITION
OF
SONG BOOKS.
A NEW SERIES, CONTAINING

Songs of the highest class, Popular, Standard, and Classical,
ALL WITH PIANOFORTE ACCOMPANIMENTS AND ENGLISH WORDS.

Price 2s. 6d. *each volume, paper cover ; also in handsome limp cover, gilt edges,* 4s., *or elegantly bound in Red Morocco, limp,* 7s.

SOPRANO SONGS [42].* BARITONE SONGS [46].*
MEZZO-SOPRANO SONGS [46].* TENOR SONGS [43].*
CONTRALTO SONGS [49].* BASS SONGS [43].*
TSCHAIKOWSKY'S SONGS [44];
With English words by FRED J. WHISHAW.

* In these six volumes, the Songs by German, French, and Italian Composers have the original words in addition to the English translations.

ENGLISH TRADITIONAL SONGS AND CAROLS.
Collected and Edited with annotations and pianoforte accompaniments. By LUCY E. BROADWOOD. Price 2s. 6d. net; also in limp cover, gilt edges, 4s. net; or, very elegantly bound in red morocco, limp, 7s. net.

RHYTHMIC SERIES.
THE NATIONAL SONG BOOK ;
A complete collection of the Folk Songs, Carols and Rounds, suggested by the Board of Education for the use of schools, edited and arranged by CHARLES VILLIERS STANFORD.

	s.	d.
Vocal score, paper cover .. .. .. Net	3	0
Do. limp, gilt .. .. .. „	4	6
Edition with words and voice parts only (in Old Notation and Tonic Sol-fa), paper cover. Net	0	9
Ditto, ditto, cloth. „	1	0

English Songs *only*, 3d. Net. Irish Songs *only*, 3d. Net.
Scotch Songs „ 3d. „ Welsh Songs „ 3d. „
Carols, Rounds, and Catches, Twopence Net.

Edition with words only .. .. .. „	0	6

A GOLDEN TREASURY OF SONG.
Price of each volume, paper cover 2s. 6d.; limp, gilt, 4s.; limp morocco, 7s.

Volumes I. and II. contain unique collections of Gems, all within moderate compass; recommended for use in Families and Schools.

Volume III. contains choice collection of Part-Songs for Female Voices (Two, Three, and Four-Part Songs), comprising a number of beautiful Works hitherto not easily accessible, together with many old favourites.

SINGING, FOR SCHOOLS AND COLLEGES ;
By WILLIAM SHAKESPEARE and HENRY F. SEARLE. Vol. I. Paper cover, 2s. 6d. ; cloth, 3s. 6d.

LIST OF CONTENTS FREE ON APPLICATION.

BOOSEY & CO., LONDON AND NEW YORK.

THE CAVENDISH MUSIC BOOKS.
PRICE ONE SHILLING EACH.   THIRTY-TWO PAGES, FULL MUSIC SIZE.

No.
1. Songs of the Day. (10). Book 1.
2. Mad. Sherrington's Ballad Concert Album. 11 Sgs.
3. Mad. A. Sterling's Ballad Concert Album. 10 Songs.
4. Mr. Sims Reeves' Ballad Concert Album. 11 Songs.
5. Mr. Santley's Ballad Concert Album. 13 Songs.
6. Album of Dance Music. Nine Sets.
7. First Pianoforte Album. Eight celebrated Pieces.
8. Second Pianoforte Album. Seven celebrated Pieces.
9. Third Pianoforte Album. Seven celebrated Pieces.
10. Fourth Pianoforte Album. 8 celebrated Pieces.
11. Madame Arabella Goddard's Pianoforte Album.
12. Fantasias, by Liszt. (3).
13. Lillie's Pianoforte Music for Young Performers.
14. First Juvenile Album. 16 Pieces for Pianoforte.
15. Sacred Airs. For Young performers on the Piano. (8).
16. Dance Music as Duets.
17. Modern Duets for Ladies' Voices. (6).
18. Modern Sacred Songs. (10).
19. Scotch Songs. (20). 1st Selection.
20. Irish Ballads. (20).
21. Old English Ballads. (20). 1st Selection.
22. Album of National Dances. 93 Country Dances, &c.
23. Moore's Irish Melodies. (68). For Pianoforte.
24. Mr. E. Lloyd's First Ballad Concert Album.
25. Duets for Men's Voices. (6).
26. Classical Readings for the Pianoforte. (17).
27. Sacred Readings for the Pianoforte. (21).
28. Recollections of the Opera, for Pianoforte. (Book 1). 26 Pieces.
29. Gavotte Album. 1st Selection. Twelve Gavottes.
30. Fifth Pianoforte Album. Eight Popular Pieces.
31. Songs of the Day. (10). Book 2.
32. Songs of the Day. (10). Book 3.
33. Album of Marches as Duets. (10).
34. Minuet Album. 18 Minuets.
35. Humorous Songs for the Drawing Room. (12).
36. Schumann's Duet Album for Young Performers.
37. Callcott's Handel Album. Part 1. 57 Oratorio Airs for Pianoforte.
38. Callcott's Handel Album. (Part 2). 61 Opera Airs for Pianoforte.
39. Overtures as Duets. (3). 1st Selection.
40. Album of National Dances of Europe. (34).
41. Boccaccio and Mascotte Dance Album.
42. Album of Old Dances. (18).
43. Album of Polonaises. (12).
44. Popular Pieces for Young Performers. (9).
45. Second Juvenile Album. 15 Pieces for Pianoforte.
46. Songs of the Day. (10). Book 4.
47. Sir Arthur Sullivan's Songs. (8).
48. Mendelssohn's Songs Without Words. (Bks. 1, 2, 3.)
49. Mendelssohn's Songs Without Words. (Bks. 4, 5, 6.)
50. Duets for Soprano and Contralto, by Hatton. (6)
51. Sixth Pianoforte Album. Seven celebrated pieces.
52. Half-hours with Offenbach and Audran. As Duets for the Pianoforte, by Callcott and de Vilbac.
53. Short Pieces for Pianoforte. (10).
54. Pieces by A. P. Wyman. (7).
55. Operatic Fantasias by Kuhe & Favarger. (4).
56. Pieces by Schulhoff. (5).
57. Pieces by Gottschalk. (6). 1st Selection.
58. Standard Overtures. (4). Book 1.
59. Pieces by C. D. Blake. (7).
60. Marches by American Composers. (10). Bk. 1.
61. Third Juvenile Album. 16 Pieces for Pianoforte.
62. March Album. Twelve celebrated Marches.
63. Popular Pieces for the Pianoforte. (8).
64. Popular Baritone Songs. (10).
65. New Baritone Songs. (10);
66. Pianoforte Duets by Volkmann. 12 Pieces.
67. Standard Overtures. (4). Book 2.
68. Songs of the Day. (10). Book 5.
69. Songs and Hymns for Sunday Evening. (46).
70. Seventh Pianoforte Album. Eleven Pieces.
71. American Ballads. (14). 1st Selection.
72. Pieces by Gottschalk. (7). 2nd selection.
73. Vocal Duets by Mendelssohn and Rubinstein. 11)
74. Waltzes by Strauss, Lanner, & Labitzky. (48).
75. American Pieces for Pianoforte. (9). 1st Selection.
76. American Ballads. (14). 2nd Selection.

No.
77. Songs for Young Girls. (18).
78. Songs of the Day. (10). Book 6.
79. Short American Pieces. (9). 2nd Selection.
80. Pieces by Sir W. Sterndale Bennett. (8).
81. Old English Ballads. (20). 2nd Selection.
82. Scotch Songs. (20). 2nd Selection.
83. Welsh Songs (Welsh and English words). (18).
84. Rubinstein's Songs (German & English words.) (12).
85. Songs by Sir W. S. Bennett & other Composers (11).
86. Schumann's First Album for the Young. (43 Characteristic Pieces).
87. Schumann's Fantasie-Stücke, Op. 12. (8 Pieces).
88. Schumann's Waldscenen, Op. 82, & Papillons, Op. 2.
89. Beethoven's & Mozart's Celebrated Waltzes. (50).
90. Album of Newest Dance Music. (8 Sets).
91. Clementi's Nine Sonatinas.
92. Gavotte Album. 2nd Selection. (18 Gavottes).
93. Smallwood's Dance Album for Young Folks.
94. Celebrated Opera-Bouffe Songs. (11).
95. Chopin's Best Pianoforte Pieces. (8). Book 1.
96. Chopin's Best Pianoforte Pieces. (11). Book 2.
97. Sankey Lover's Songs.
98. Gounod's Songs. (10).
99. Fahrbach's Polkas. (16).
100. American Ballads. (15). 3rd Selection.
101. American Pieces for Pianoforte. (12). 3rd Sel.
102. Oratorio Gems. 16 Popular Songs. 1st Selection.
103. Songs of the Day. (10). Book 7.
104. Duets for Ladies' Voices. (7).
105. Smallwood's Juvenile Duet Album for Piano.
106. "Maritana" and "The Bohemian Girl." The Principal Airs arranged for Pianoforte.
107. Marzials' Album. 9 Songs by Theo. Marzials.
108. Eighth Pianoforte Album. Eight Pieces.
109. National Anthems of all Nations for Piano.
110. Fourth Juvenile Album. 15 Pieces for Pianoforte.
111. Oratorio Gems (Songs). 2nd Selection.
112. Standard Tenor Songs. (12).
113. Short Pieces for the Pianoforte, by Mendelssohn and Beethoven.
114. Madame Belle Cole's Concert Album. 13 Songs.
115. Standard Soprano Songs (8).
116. Overtures as Duets (3). 2nd Selection.
117. Popular English Ballads (12).
118. Standard Bass Songs (10). 1st Selection.
119. American Songs. (10). 4th Selection.
120. Sacred Gems from Mendelssohn. (16). For Piano.
121. Smallwood's American Dance Album. 16 Pieces.
122. Seven Songs by Blumenthal.
123. Standard Vocal Duets. (6).
124. Popular Duets for Ladies' Voices. (8).
125. Hatton's Songs (12). Words by Herrick & Ben Jonson.
126. Boosey's Dance Album. (Thine Alone Valse, &c.)*
127. Songs by Tschaikowsky (12), with English Words.
128. Miss E. Florence's Concert Album. 10 Songs.
129. Fifth Juvenile Album. 17 Pieces for Pianoforte.
130. Recollections of the Opera, for Pianoforte. Book 2. 18 Pieces.
131. Mr. E. Lloyd's Second Ballad Concert Album.
132. Standard Bass Songs (7). 2nd Selection.
133. Marches by American Composers. (13). Bk. 2.
134. Easy Pieces for the Pianoforte (12) By A. Renaud
135. Songs of the Day. (8). Book 8.
136. Balfe Album of Songs and Duets. (7).
137. Christmas Dance Album. (1898).*
138. Regimental Marches. (58).
139. Russian Melodies (15). For the Pianoforte.
140. Popular English Songs. (9).
141. Chopin's Eight Valses. Edited by E. Horne.
142. Chopin's Nocturnes. Complete, edited by E. Horne.
143. Original Pieces for the Pianoforte, for young performers. Tschaikowsky.
144. Album of American Marches. Standard and Popular.
145. Standard and Popular Contralto Songs
146. Standard and Popular Baritone Songs.
147. Six Songs by Schubert, transcribed for Pianoforte by M. Kuhe.
148. Thirteen Famous Songs by Clairibel.
149. Easy Pieces for the Piano (10). 2nd Set, A. Renaud.

* Violin Parts of Nos. 126 and 137. Sixpence each.   *** *A detailed List of contents sent on application.*

BOOSEY & CO., 295, REGENT STREET, LONDON, W., and 9, EAST 17th STREET, NEW YORK.

OPERAS AND OPERETTAS.

		s. d.			s. d.
Shamus O'Brien	... Stanford	5 0	Indiana	... Audran	5 0
Ma Mie Rosette	... Caryll and Lacome	5 0	Grand Mogul	Audran	6 0
The Basoche	Messager	6 0	Pot-Pourri	Lambelet	6 0
Esmeralda	Thomas	6 0	Royal Star	Clerice	6 0
Nadeshda	Thomas	6 0	Boccaccio...	... Von Suppe	5 0
Veiled Prophet	Stanford	7 6	La Vie	Offenbach	5 0
Canterbury Pilgrims... ...	Stanford	6 0	Perichole	Offenbach	5 0
Sigurd	Reyer	12 0	Peter the Shipwright ...	Lortzing	5 0
Beggar-Student...	Millöcker	5 0	The Chieftain	Sullivan	5 0
Pauline	Cowen	7 6	Love and Law	Caryll	2 6
Diarmid	McCunn	7 6	Venetian Singer	Jakobowski	3 0

DRAWING-ROOM OPERETTAS.
With dialogue and stage directions.

	s. d.		s. d.
†*The Goose Girl, a Musical Play for the Young (Eight Solo Parts and Chorus) A. Scott-Gatty	3 0	Good-Night, Babette, Musical Idyll Liza Lehmann	4 0
†*Rumpelstiltskin, a Musical Play for the Young (Six Solo Parts and Chorus) A. Scott-Gatty	3 0	Olla Podrida, an Operatic Charade (for Treble or Mixed Voices) ... ... Louis Diehl	2 6
		†A Dress Rehearsal (12 F.) ... Louis Diehl	2 6
†*The Three Bears, a Musical Play for the Young (Ten Solo Parts and Chorus) A. Scott-Gatty	3 0	†Coquette (3 M., 4 F., and Chorus) Sopwith and Rawlinson	3 0
		*Pickwick (2 M., 2 F.) ... ... E. Solomon	2 6
L. S. D. Musical Charade (2 M., 1 F.) A Scott-Gatty	0 6	†Paquerette (1 M., 3 F.) ... Offenbach	2 6
		Cox and Box (3 M.) ... Arthur Sullivan	2 6
Elsa's Fairy, a Musical Play for Girls (Four Solo Parts and Chorus) Myles B. Foster	1 0	An Adamless Eden (17 F.) ... W. Slaughter	2 6
		The Enchanted Island (3 M., 2 F.) R. H. Walthew	3 0
†The Wooden Spoon, (2 M., 2 F.) Hope Temple	2 6	Fact and Fancy (2 M., 2 F.) .. G. H. Stone	2 6
		Dream Lovers (2 M., 2 F.) S. Coleridge-Taylor	2 6

(M. = Male characters. F. = Female characters.)
* Separate Librettos can be had. † Band Parts can be had from the Publishers.

BOOSEY'S CABINET OPERAS FOR PIANOFORTE.
The Numbers refer to the Musical Cabinet.

ONE SHILLING EACH.

Ballo in Maschera (60)	Verdi	Guillaume Tell (125)	Rossini
Barbiere di Siviglia (109)	Rossini	Jolie Parfumeuse (181)	Offenbach
Brigands (151)	Offenbach	Lucia di Lammermoor (142) ...	Donizetti
Crispino e la Comare (92)	Ricci	Lucrezia Borgia (111)	Donizetti
Dame Blanche (175)	Boieldieu	Martha (108)	Flotow
Diamans de la Couronne (127) ...	Auber	Masaniello (128)	Auber
Domino Noir (123)	Auber	Norma (107)	Bellini
Don Pasquale (122)	Donizetti	Oberon (202)	Weber
Don Juan (112)	Mozart	Périchole (150)	Offenbach
Ernani (176)	Verdi	Princess of Trebizonde (149) ...	Offenbach
Favorita (177)	Donizetti	Rigoletto (119)	Verdi
Fidelio (110)	Beethoven	Robert le Diable (115)	Meyerbeer
Figaro (118)	Mozart	Satanella (182)	Balfe
Figlia del Reggimento (178) ...	Donizetti	Semiramide (183)	Rossini
Fille de Madame Angot (179) ...	Lecocq	Sonnambula (104)	Bellini
Flauto Magico (180)	Mozart	Traviata (41)	Verdi
Fra Diavolo (126)	Auber	Trovatore (40)	Verdi
Freischütz (105)	Weber	Zampa (124)	Herold
Geneviève de Brabant (154) ...	Offenbach		

DOUBLE NUMBERS.

		s. d.			s. d.
Grand Duchess...	Offenbach	2 6	Vêpres Siciliennes (185) ...	Verdi	2 0
Mirella	Gounod	2 6	La Mascotte	Audran	2 6
Dinorah (184)	Meyerbeer	2 0	Nadeshda	A. G. Thomas	3 0
Flying Dutchman (199) ...	Wagner	2 0	The Beggar-Student... ...	Millöcker	2 6
Huguenots (185)	Meyerbeer	2 0	The Basoche	Messager	3 0
Lohengrin (186)...	Wagner	2 0	Ma Mie Rosette ...	Lacome and Caryll	3 0
Boccaccio	Von Suppe	2 0	The Chieftain	Sullivan	3 0
Tannhäuser (187)	Wagner	2 0	Shamus O'Brien	Stanford	3 0

BOOSEY'S GUIDE TO THE OPERA, containing the Plots and incidents of a great number of the well-known standard Operas, with short sketches of the lives of the Composers. Price 2s. 6d., cloth.

LONDON: BOOSEY & CO., 295, REGENT STREET, W.
And 9, EAST 17th STREET, NEW YORK.

THE ROYAL SONG BOOKS.

Price 2s. 6d. each, in paper covers; 4s. in cloth, gilt edges.

Songs of England. (281). In 3 Vols.
EDITED BY J. L. HATTON AND EATON FANING.

Songs of Scotland. (333). In 2 Vols.
EDITED BY COLIN BROWN, J. PITTMAN, MYLES B. FOSTER, & DR. CHARLES MACKAY.

Songs of Ireland. (108).
EDITED BY J. L. HATTON AND J. L. MOLLOY, Including Seventy-eight of Moore's Irish Melodies and Thirty National Songs.

Songs of Wales. (69).
With Welsh and English Words.
EDITED BY BRINLEY RICHARDS.

Manx National Songs. (51).
With English Words, Selected from the MS. Collection of THE DEEMSTER GILL, DR. J. CLAGUE, and W. H. GILL, and arranged by W. H. GILL.

Songs of France. (61).
With French and English Words.

Songs of Germany. (100).
With German and English Words.
EDITED BY J. A. KAPPEY.

Songs of Italy. (54).
Conti. Popolari and Modern Italian Songs, with Italian and English Words.

Songs of Scandinavia and Northern Europe. (83).
National & Popular Songs, with English Words only
EDITED BY J. A. KAPPEY.

Songs of Eastern Europe. (100).
EDITED BY J. A. KAPPEY.
Volkslieder of Austria, Hungary, Bohemia, Servia, &c., with English Words only.

Mozart's Songs. (37).
With German, Italian, and English Words.

Beethoven's Songs. (76).
With German and English Words.

Mendelssohn's Songs & Duets. (60).
EDITED BY J. PITTMAN.
Fifty-four Songs, and the Six Popular Duets, Op. 63, with German and English Words.

Schumann's Songs. (75).
With German and English Words.
EDITED BY J. L. HATTON.

Schubert's Songs. (115). In 2 Vols.
With German and English Words.
EDITED BY J. A. KAPPEY & MYLES B. FOSTER.

Rubinstein's Songs. (59).
With German and English Words. New and enlarged edition.

Rubinstein's Duets. (18).
With German and English Words.
EDITED BY HERMANN EISOLDT.

Handel's Oratorio Songs. (55).
EDITED BY W. T. BEST.

Handel's Opera Songs (52).
With Italian and English Words.
EDITED BY W. T. BEST.

Songs from the Oratorios. (49).
EDITED BY MYLES B. FOSTER.
Selected from the most famous works of Handel, Mendelssohn, Haydn, Rossini, Bach, Spohr, and Arthur Sullivan.

Songs from the Operas.
A collection of popular Operatic Songs, transposed into medium keys. In Two Vols., price 2s. 6d. each, paper covers, 4s. cloth, gilt edges. Each Book contains 50 Songs, with Italian and English Words.
Vol. I. Mezzo-Soprano and Contralto.
Vol. II.—Tenor and Baritone.

Modern Ballads. (50).
By Sullivan, Pinsuti, Molloy, Cowen, Gabriel, Gatty, Marzials, Aidé, Claribel, &c., &c.

Sacred Songs. (101).
EDITED BY JOHN HILES.
By the most celebrated Ancient and Modern Composers, and including several new compositions.

Humorous Songs. (72).
EDITED BY J. L. HATTON.
New and Popular Social Songs by Offenbach, Lecocq, Sullivan, Hatton, H. J. Byron, Hood, Hook, Blewitt, Bayly, &c.

Duets for Ladies' Voices. (24).
EDITED BY RANDEGGER.
Choice Duets by Handel, Rossini, Bishop, Haydn, Sullivan, Balfe, Mendelssohn, &c., &c.

Albums of Operatic Duets.
Vol. I.—20 Duets, Soprano and Mezzo-Soprano.
Vol. II.—20 Duets, Soprano and Contralto.
Each, 2s. 6d. paper cover, 4s. cloth. Vols. I. and II. in one book, 5s. paper cover, 7s. 6d. cloth gilt.

Double Volumes.
THE ROYAL OPERATIC ALBUMS.

Price 6s. each, paper covers; 7s. 6d. cloth, gilt edges.

The most comprehensive collection of Dramatic Music ever published, containing 186 Celebrated Songs, Scenas, &c., from renowned Operas, including several hitherto unknown in England.
All the songs, &c., have Italian and English words, and are published in the original keys, without alteration.

Vol. I.—The Prima Donna's Album.
40 Songs for Soprano.

Vol. II.—The Contralto Album.
50 Songs for Mezzo-Soprano or Contralto.

Vol. III.—The Tenor Album.
50 Songs for Tenor.

Vol. IV.—The Baritone Album.
45 Songs for Baritone.

LONDON: BOOSEY & CO., 295, REGENT STREET, W.,
And 9 EAST 17th STREET, NEW YORK.